Healthy Me

MAKE GOOD CHOICES

Your Guide to Making Healthy Decisions

By Heather E. Schwartz

Consultant:
Jennifer F. Le, MD
Department of Psychiatry
Division of Child and Adolescent Psychiatry
University of Louisville School of Medicine

CAPSTONE PRESS
a capstone imprint

Snap Books are published by Capstone Press,
151 Good Counsel Drive, P.O. Box 669, Mankato, Minnesota 56002.
www.capstonepub.com

Books published by Capstone Press are manufactured with paper
containing at least 10 percent post-consumer waste.

Library of Congress Cataloging-in-Publication Data
Schwartz, Heather E.
Make good choices : your guide to making healthy decisions/ by Heather E. Schwartz.
p. cm.—(Snap. Healthy me.)
Includes bibliographical references and index.
Summary: "An introduction to making healthy choices, including the dangers of tobacco, alcohol, and
drugs"—Provided by publisher.
ISBN 978-1-4296-6546-9 (library binding)
ISBN 978-1-4296-7295-5 (paperback)
1. Decision making—Juvenile literature. I. Title.
BF448.S393 2012
153.8'3—dc22
2011009811

Editorial Credits:
Lori Shores, editor; Juliette Peters, designer; Svetlana Zhurkin, media researcher; Sarah Schuette, photo stylist;
    Marcy Morin, studio scheduler; Laura Manthe, production specialist

Photo Credits:
Capstone Studio: Karon Dubke, 5, 6, 7, 9, 10, 12, 13, 14, 15, 17, 18, 21, 22, 26, 28; Image Farm, 23 (signs); iStockphoto:
Camilla Wisbauer, cover (right); Shutterstock: Andresr, 29, Artpose Adam Borkowski, cover (front), Stillfx, cover (top
left); Svetlana Zhurkin, cover (bottom left)

Essential content terms are **bold** and are defined at the bottom of the page where they first appear.

Printed in the United States of America in North Mankato, Minnesota.
032011   006110CGF11

Table of Contents

Chapter 1

Decisions, Decisions

From the moment your alarm goes off, your day of decision making has begun. Should you get right out of bed or close your eyes for a little longer? After a little extra snooze time, you race to the shower. Your choice to sleep in had **consequences**. Now you really have to hurry.

You dress quickly and gain some more time. Should you eat a quick breakfast or check your e-mail? Your stomach growls, and you choose breakfast. You know you won't be able to concentrate in class with an empty stomach.

At school you're faced with choice after choice. Should you raise your hand in class? You don't, but you regret it when you realize you had the right answer. Should you strike up a conversation with the new kid? You take a chance with good results. It turns out you have a lot in common.

Later in the day, you face more difficult decisions. Your friends want you to skip soccer practice to go to a movie. But if you skip, you might not get to play in Saturday's game.

consequence: the result of an action

Healthy Tip

Happiness is also a choice. Choosing to keep a positive attitude can make a big difference in your day.

It's Complicated

On the way to practice, you catch some bullies teasing a younger student. Should you step in? Tell someone? You're afraid of the bullies, so you pretend not to notice. The decision doesn't feel good, though. In fact, you feel so guilty that you don't want to go to soccer practice anymore. Now you're getting confused. Would skipping practice make you feel better? Or worse?

You make decisions all day long. When things are going smoothly, it's like breezing through an easy multiple-choice test. Everyday decisions might not seem very important. You could be late if you hit the snooze button, but you'll get there. You might be hungry if you skip breakfast, but you can have a snack. Right?

But lately life has gotten complicated. You're not always sure what to do. Keeping an eye on possible consequences helps you face tough choices. Being late to school too often could lower your grades. Skipping breakfast every day could harm your health. Considering the pros and cons can keep you from making a poor choice.

Chapter 2

Making the Right Choice

Sometimes the right choice is plain to see. In many cases, you probably make choices between following or breaking rules. You might not even realize you're making a choice. Maybe you hand in your homework on time without a second thought. You know handing it in late would affect your grade.

What if you're in a situation without set rules? Suppose that you get a strange e-mail from an unknown sender. Maybe there's no rule that you can't open or answer it, but what might happen if you do? You could end up with a computer virus. Worse, the sender might be someone dangerous. When there's a decision to be made, take time to think it through. Good choices keep you safe, healthy, and out of trouble. Choose the options that will protect you and your future.

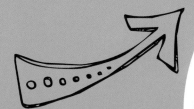

Healthy Tip

You don't always have to choose one way or the other with no in-between. If the options would put you at risk, you don't have to choose any of them. Parents, teachers, and other trusted adults can help you find positive alternatives.

When you're faced with a difficult decision, don't worry. You can make a smart choice with a little know-how. Making a decision is a **process**, like brushing your teeth. Take it step-by-step, and you'll come out smiling.

Suppose you promise to babysit for a neighbor, but later you're invited to a birthday party. What should you do? First, gather some information. What time will your neighbors come home? Could you do both by arriving late to the party? Could someone else babysit for you? Who will be at the party? Gathering information will help you identify your options.

process: an organized series of actions that produce a result

Next, consider the consequences. If you cancel on your neighbors, they might not hire you again. If you babysit, you'll have cash for the weekend. Plus, you will have kept a promise.

If you attend the party, you might have fun. But there might be alcohol at the party, which would make you uncomfortable. Worse, you could get into trouble.

Evaluating your options makes it easer to make the right choice. It's your chance to ask yourself which option would be the best one for you.

evaluate: to judge or determine the value of something

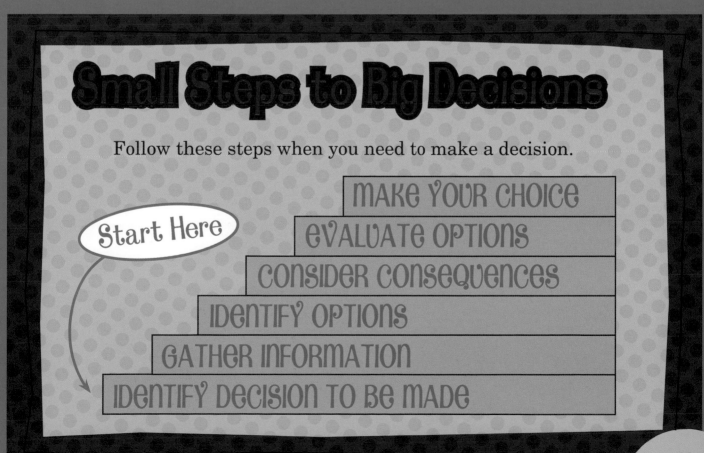

Small Steps to Big Decisions

Follow these steps when you need to make a decision.

MAKE YOUR CHOICE

Start Here

EVALUATE OPTIONS

CONSIDER CONSEQUENCES

IDENTIFY OPTIONS

GATHER INFORMATION

IDENTIFY DECISION TO BE MADE

When Good Choices Feel Bad

Making good choices can get confusing. Sometimes the right choices don't feel very good. Suppose you decide to study for a test instead of hanging out with friends. You know you're doing the right thing. But it's only natural to feel sad about missing the fun.

When you make good choices for your future, you sometimes have to **sacrifice** in the present. That's hard, but don't let your good choices get you down. Remind yourself why you made the decision. You'll feel good when you do well on the test. And you'll be proud of yourself when your report card reflects your hard work. You made the decision yourself even though it was difficult. You can feel good about making the right choice for you.

sacrifice: to give up something important or enjoyable for a good reason

Difficult Decisions

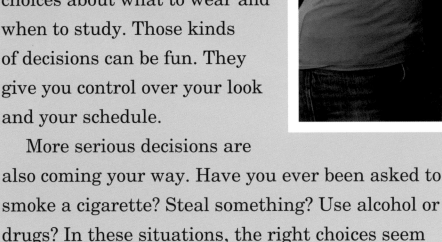

As you get older, you'll make more decisions on your own. By now, you probably make choices about what to wear and when to study. Those kinds of decisions can be fun. They give you control over your look and your schedule.

More serious decisions are also coming your way. Have you ever been asked to smoke a cigarette? Steal something? Use alcohol or drugs? In these situations, the right choices seem obvious. But when the pressure is on, it's not always easy to know what to do.

Decisions like these can be life changing, so be prepared. Knowing the facts will help you make an **informed decision**. Use the decision-making process to evaluate options ahead of time. Then when the day comes, you'll be ready to make the right choice.

informed decision: a decision made after learning facts that apply to the choices and consequences

Just the Facts

Smoking is not a good choice for anyone, but for kids it's even worse. Studies show that people who start smoking before age 21 have a harder time quitting smoking later. They also have a higher risk of dying from a smoking-related disease.

The Big Three

Alcohol use might seem OK on TV, but that's not always true. It is against the law for kids and with good reason. Alcohol can cause long-term damage to developing brains. Drinking large amounts of alcohol can also cause alcohol poisoning, which can lead to death. And alcohol is **addictive**. People who begin drinking at a young age have a higher risk of developing problems with alcohol use.

Drug use is risky for people of all ages. Illegal drugs, such as meth and cocaine, damage the brain. Marijuana, also illegal, affects learning, memory, and problem solving. Abusing prescription drugs is just as dangerous. Not all medications are safe for everyone. Only a doctor can determine what is safe for you. Even over-the-counter medicines, such as cough medicine or diet pills, can cause **seizures** and even death when abused. Many illegal drugs can kill a person, even the first time they're used. Why risk it?

addictive: very difficult to quit or give up

seizure: a sudden attack that sometimes causes a person to shake violently

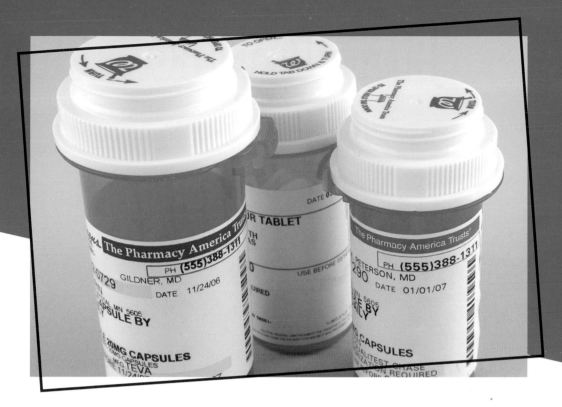

Smoking is unhealthy for everyone, but it is also against the law for kids. Using tobacco can cause many types of cancer and other diseases. Smoking also increases your chances of getting colds, flu, and bronchitis. Other consequences include bad breath and yellow teeth. Who wants that?

Healthy Tip

Despite what some people say, there are no safe ways to use tobacco. E-cigarettes, chewing, and other forms of tobacco use are all dangerous and can be deadly.

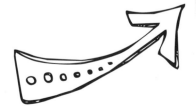

Chapter 3

Pitfalls to Poor Choices

Choices that put your health and safety in danger are never worth it. Still, kids sometimes say yes to those risks. They may believe risky activities will help them fit in or be accepted by others. They might like the idea of trying something off-limits. Other kids take big risks because they're caught off guard by a situation. Suppose you're hanging out with some new friends when someone brings out a bottle of alcohol. You didn't expect to be in this situation, but suddenly you are.

Even if you find yourself facing a decision you didn't expect, you can always weigh the risks. Ask yourself a few questions.

- *What might happen as a result?*
- *How might the activity affect me?*
- *Will the activity affect other people?*

Suppose you are on the basketball team. If you smoke cigarettes, you'll be kicked off the team. Is that risk worth it? Smoking will also harm your health. Are you willing to take that risk? If an activity might put you at risk or make you sick, say no.

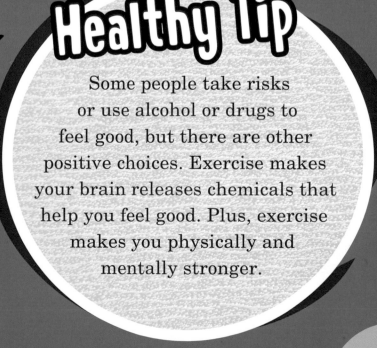

Healthy Tip

Some people take risks or use alcohol or drugs to feel good, but there are other positive choices. Exercise makes your brain releases chemicals that help you feel good. Plus, exercise makes you physically and mentally stronger.

Peer Pressure

Knowing the risks, it might seem easy to decide against dangerous activities. But what if your best friend is the one taking risks? Suppose you were at a friend's house and your friend was sneaking alcohol from the kitchen?

No matter how strong you are, your **peers** can influence how you think, act, and feel. When your teammates inspire you to train harder in a sport, that's positive peer pressure. But when your friends want you to do something you know is wrong, that's negative peer pressure. Saying no isn't always easy. You may want to please a friend or fit in with a certain crowd. But you will feel worse if you go against your **values**.

The good news is that you're not alone when it comes to peer pressure. Talk to friends who share your values. Agree to support each other when pressured to make poor choices. It's easier to stand up to peer pressure when you're not alone.

peer: a person of the same age

value: a belief or idea that is important to a person

Just the Facts

Four out of five teenagers choose not to smoke.

Sneaky Stress

Other kinds of pressure can lead to poor choices. Does school **stress** you out? Are you unhappy about a situation at home? Sometimes kids take risks when they need attention. They might not even realize that attention is the reason behind their bad choices.

Making a bad choice may sometimes seem like a good solution. Goofing off in class might help you get attention. Leaving home without telling your parents could get you a few hours of peace at a friend's house. But these kinds of solutions will only make a bad situation worse. You may have to stay after school for goofing off. You could fall behind with your homework if you don't pay attention. Your parents will be upset and worried if they think you're missing. You may be grounded and create even more stress at home.

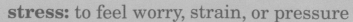

stress: to feel worry, strain, or pressure

Stress Ahead!

When you're stressed, it's hard to make good choices. Find healthy solutions by talking with your parents, a teacher, a doctor, or other trusted adults. Watch for these warning signs of stress.

poor appetite

overeating

feeling anxious

sleeping too much

trouble sleeping

grinding teeth

headaches

constant worrying

Chapter 4

Saying No

Making good choices sometimes means speaking up and speaking your mind. Often it means you have to say no. It's just a tiny, two-letter word, but it's tough for many kids to say. You might feel embarrassed or **self-conscious**. You might want to please others or fit in by saying yes instead.

Learning to say no doesn't come naturally with age. It's a struggle even for many adults. Think of different ways to say no to drugs or alcohol. A simple "No, thanks" will usually work. Or you might say, "No, I'm not into that." Start practicing now, and you'll build **confidence**. It will get easier.

self-conscious: being worried about what others are thinking about you

confidence: a strong belief in your own abilities

Just the Facts

One out of every seven kids in grades four through six has been offered drugs. Many kids practice ways of saying no so they'll be ready just in case.

You Choose!

When you say no to something, you run the risk of being left out or left behind. Sometimes it helps to say yes to something else. Choose your favorite option for each situation.

We can't be friends if I say no? OK, I'll meet new friends by . . .

becoming a volunteer.

joining the drama club.

trying out for a team.

There will be drugs at the party? I would rather . . .

go to a movie.

shoot hoops with a friend.

play a game with my family.

Smoking gives you something to do with your hands? I'd rather . . .

text.

doodle.

play guitar.

Your soda tastes great with alcohol? I'd rather add . . .

some cherries.

a slice of lemon.

a scoop of ice cream.

You think I'm weird for saying no? I think I'm . . .

confident.

strong.

unique.

It's Your Right

It doesn't really matter why you choose to say no to something. You always have the right to say no. Friends may ask why you're not joining in. Others might think you feel like you're better than they are. At the worst, someone might make fun of you. But when you're protecting yourself and your health, you can be confident in your choice. It doesn't matter what others say. Always stick to what is right for you.

You can also send the same message without saying a word. Skip parties where you know alcohol will be served. Spend time with friends who don't smoke instead of with those that do. You don't have to stop being their friend. But sometimes just being with people who are smoking or drinking can have consequences, even if you don't join in.

When it comes to standing up for yourself and making good choices, you're not alone. If you are struggling with peer pressure, don't hesitate to find help. You can always turn to parents, teachers, doctors, and other trusted adults for help.

Healthy Tip

You don't have to explain yourself, but it can help to have a response ready. Be consistent in your message and people should accept what you say.

Creating Your Future

Making good choices isn't just about saying no to tobacco, alcohol, and other drugs. Those are important issues, but every decision counts. You're learning to take care of yourself and to do what's best for you. Even poor choices sometimes help you learn to do better next time.

It's not always easy to make good choices and stick with them. But it's worth the effort. Whether big or small, your good choices help you create more than a good day. They add up to a solid foundation for a great future.

Glossary

addictive (uh-DIK-tiv)—very difficult to quit or give up

confidence (KON-fuh-dense)—a strong belief in your own abilities

consequence (KAHN-suh-kwens)—the result of an action

evaluate (i-VAL-yoo-ate)—to judge or determine the value of something

informed decision (in-FORMD di-SIZH-uhn)—a decision made after learning facts that apply to the choices and consequences

peer (PIHR)—a person of the same age or rank

process (PROH-sess)—an organized series of actions that produce a result

sacrifice (SAK-ruh-fise)—to give up something important or enjoyable for a good reason

seizure (SEE-zhur)—a sudden attack that sometimes causes a person to shake violently

self-conscious (self-KON-shuhss)—being worried about what others are thinking about you

stress (STRESS)—to feel worry, strain, or pressure

value (VAL-yoo)—a belief or idea that is important to a person

Read More

Anderson, W. M. *Talking about Making Good Choices.*
Healthy Living. New York: Gareth Stevens Pub., 2010.

Giddens, Sandra, and Owen Giddens. *Making
Smart Choices about Cigarettes, Drugs, and Alcohol.*
Making Smart Choices. New York: Rosen Pub., 2008.

Moss, Wendy L. *Being Me: A Kid's Guide to Boosting
Confidence and Self-Esteem.* Washington, D.C.:
Magination Press, 2011.

Internet Sites

FactHound offers a safe, fun way to find Internet
sites related to this book. All of the sites on
FactHound have been researched by our staff.

Here's all you do:

Visit *www.facthound.com*

Type in this code: 9781429665469

 Check out projects, games and lots more at
www.capstonekids.com

Index